Read

AGE 3-5

Sue Barraclough
Educational consultant: Margaret Deehan
Illustrated by Emma Holt

This workbook is designed to set your child on the road to reading. It will help them learn the following skills and concepts, all of which are essential parts of reading:

- **understanding that each letter has a sound**

- **recognising different letter shapes, especially distinguishing between similar letters like p and q and b and d**

- **familiarity with common strings of letters and words**

- **recognising word shapes**

- **discovering that letters and words are all around them and enjoying the excitement of exploring and understanding them.**

How to help your child

- Keep sessions short (no more than 20 minutes) and regular.
- The exercises are intended to be enjoyable as well as educational. It is important that your child sees that learning is fun, so always stop if they are not relaxed or have lost concentration.
- Build confidence. Offer praise and encouragement for the smallest efforts. The exercises are very simple, but they are a real challenge for a young child. It is essential that they acquire these basic skills thoroughly.
- Have at least four different coloured pens or pencils to do the exercises. Children will be able to see clearly what they have achieved, and picking up and putting down the different pens is good practice in itself.
- When you read the instructions to your child, run your finger along the sentence from left to right, so they become used to the movement of reading.
- Point out the difference between long and short words, and help your child to notice shapes and patterns within words.

Hodder Children's Books

The only home learning programme supported by the NCPTA

Before you begin

It is important as you go through this book that you describe the letters correctly for your child. Say the sound of each letter, rather than its name. For example, say 'duh' and not 'dee' for letter d, 'fuh' and not 'eff' for letter f and so on. The pictures below will help you with the correct sounds for each letter of the alphabet.

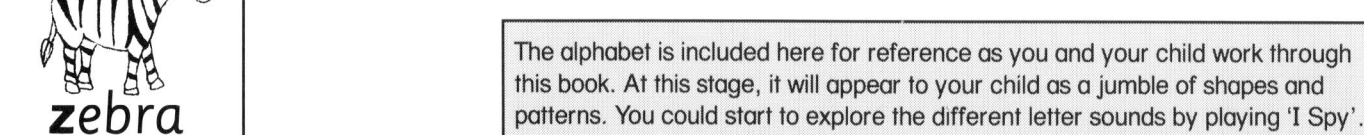

apple	**b**alloon	**c**at	**d**uck	**e**gg
fish	**g**oose	**h**orse	**i**gloo	**j**elly
kite	**l**emon	**m**onster	**n**est	**o**range
pig	**q**ueen	**r**abbit	**s**un	**t**eapot
umbrella	**v**an	**w**atch	fo**x**	**y**o-yo
zebra				

The alphabet is included here for reference as you and your child work through this book. At this stage, it will appear to your child as a jumble of shapes and patterns. You could start to explore the different letter sounds by playing 'I Spy'.

Match up

Draw a line to join each pair of look-alike fish.

Learning to look closely at pictorial shapes and patterns will help children develop the ability to recognise different letter and word shapes. You could continue the exercise by asking your child to colour the stripy fish red, the spotty fish green and the bubbles blue.

Odd one out

Colour the odd one out in each row. Then use a different colour for the other shapes.

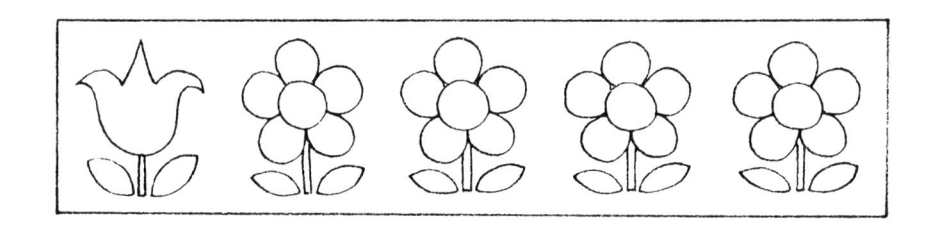

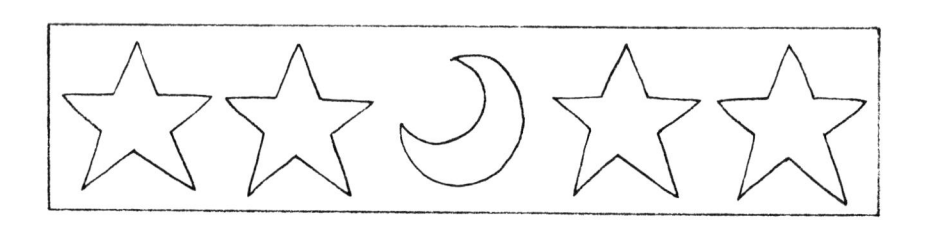

This exercise encourages your child to look carefully at patterns and shapes. The colouring will also help with pencil control.

Patterns

Look at the pattern in each row. Can you work out which picture or shape should come next? Colour it in.

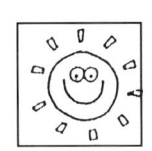

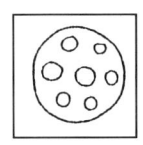

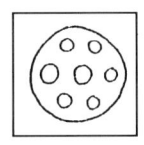

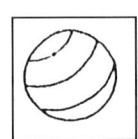

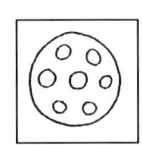

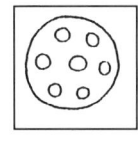

What comes next in these patterns? Draw the right shape in the empty box.

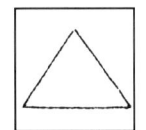

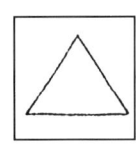

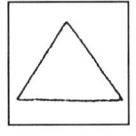

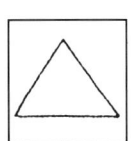

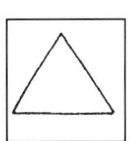

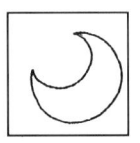

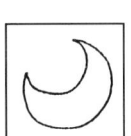

This exercise prepares children for recognising letter patterns. It will also help them get used to the left-to-right movement of reading. Your child may find it easier to see the pattern if they say the name of each object as they move along the line.

Fish for letters!

Find the right letters in the fish tanks, and draw a ring round them.

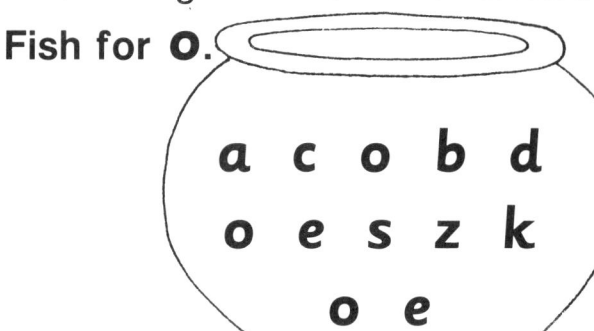

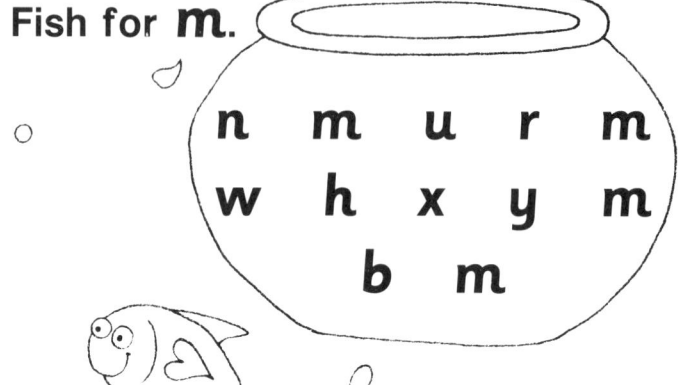

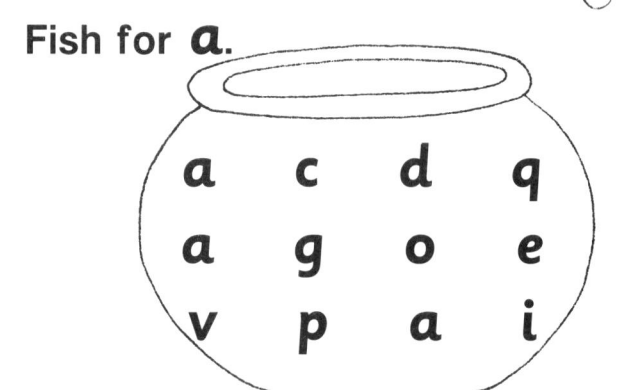

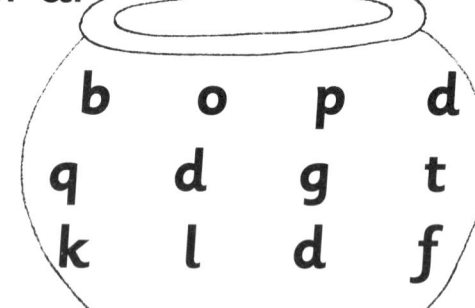

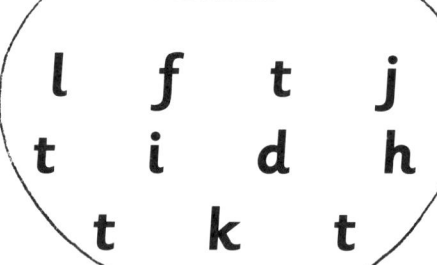

Fish for **o**.

a c o b d
o e s z k
o e

Fish for **m**.

n m u r m
w h x y m
b m

Fish for **a**.

a c d q
a g o e
v p a i

Fish for **d**.

b o p d
q d g t
k l d f

Fish for **p**.

p b d p
q p g o
a y p n

Fish for **t**.

l f t j
t i d h
t k t

This page moves on from shapes and pictures to recognising actual letters. You can continue this exercise by asking children to spot particular letters on cereal packets, or in the text of a picture book.

Colouring by letter

Colour the juggler's clothes using the letter code.

b blue
g green
r red
y yellow

Help your child to colour the blobs in the code correctly to start them off. Explain that the letter b on the juggler's sleeve means you should colour it blue, and so on. This exercise will improve pencil control as well as letter recognition.

Letter shapes

Look at the shape and guess what its label says. Look for matching letters inside the shape, and join each pair of letters with a line.

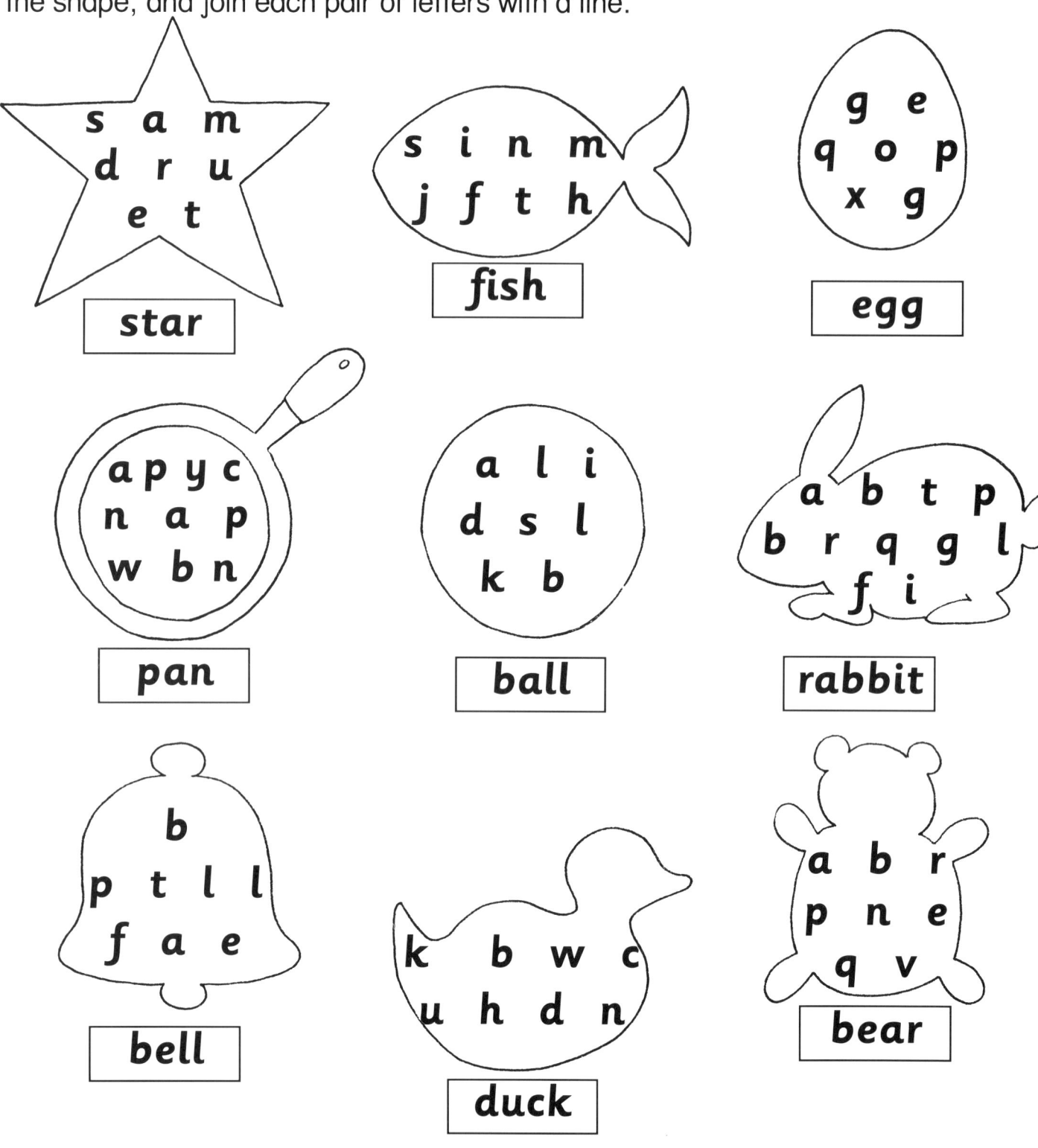

s a m
d r u
e t

star

s i n m
j f t h

fish

g e
q o p
x g

egg

a p y c
n a p
w b n

pan

a l i
d s l
k b

ball

a b t p
b r q g l
f i

rabbit

b
p t l l
f a e

bell

k b w c
u h d n

duck

a b r
p n e
q v

bear

This is a simple letter matching exercise. Your child will also be learning how letters join together to make words.

First letters

Look at each picture. Say its name and listen for the first letter sound. Draw a ring round the letter with the same sound.

(boat) a b c	(dog) d e f	(house) g h i
(leaf) j k l	(mouse) m n o	(penguin) p q r
(tortoise) s t u	(windmill) v w x	(zip) y z a
(cow) b c d	(gate) e f g	(jug) h i j
(lemon) l m o	(robot) p q r	(umbrella) s t u

Children can often recognise letters long before they can write them. Your child may find it helpful to look back at page 2, 'Before you begin'.

Word trail

Read the word under each picture. Then draw a line to join all the words which are the same. Use a different colour for each one.

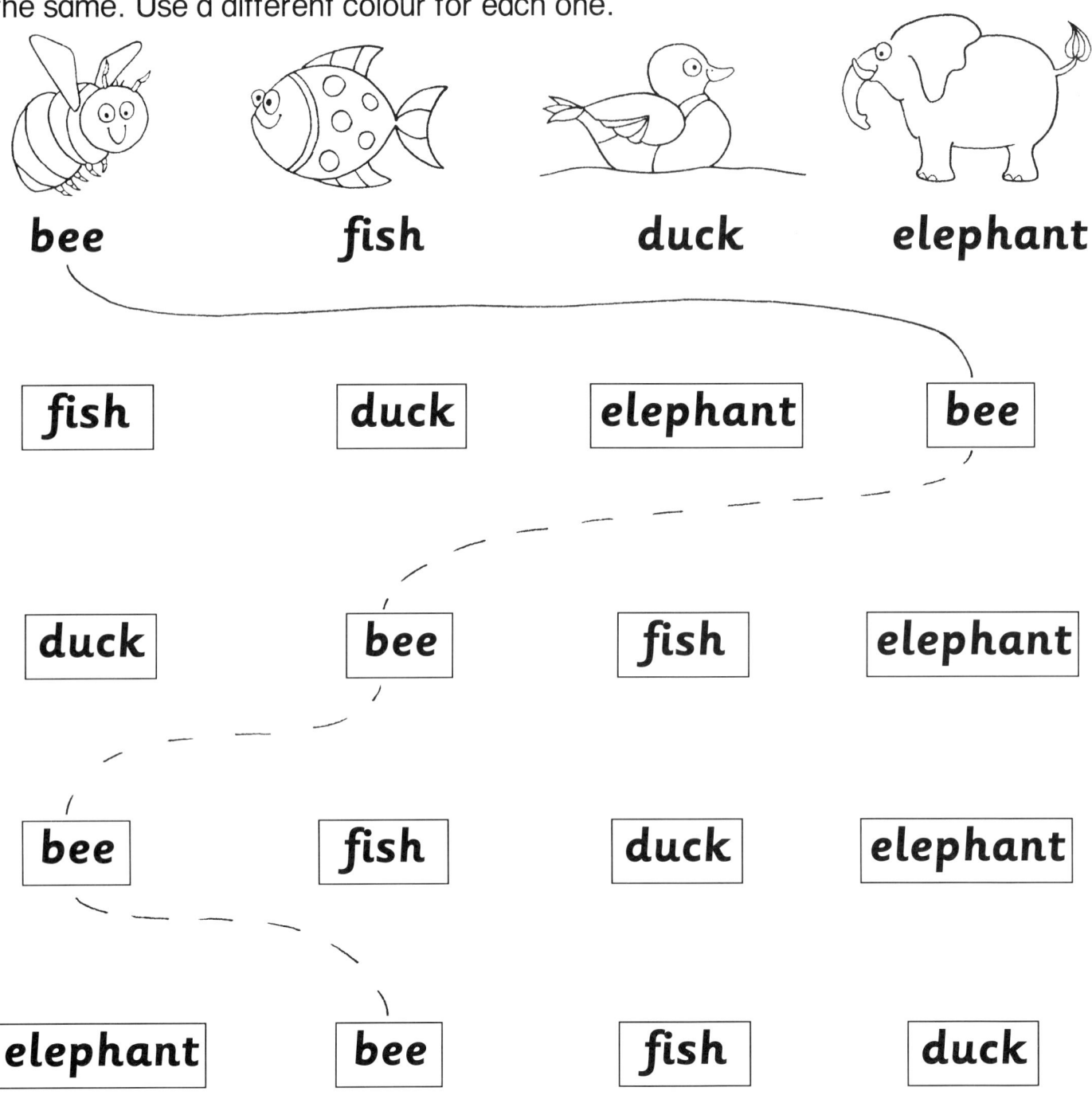

bee   fish   duck   elephant

| fish | duck | elephant | bee |

| duck | bee | fish | elephant |

| bee | fish | duck | elephant |

| elephant | bee | fish | duck |

This is a matching exercise, which will also help your child to become used to different shapes of letters combined into words. Point out the difference between long and short words.

Odd word out

There is an odd word out in each row. Ring it with a red crayon when you find it.

fish fish fish dish fish fish fish

carrot carrot parrot carrot carrot

cat cat cat hat cat cat cat cat cat

mouse mouse mouse house mouse

car car car jar car car car car

pear bear pear pear pear pear pear

cow bow bow bow bow bow bow

Words that are quite similar in formation have been chosen here, so that your child will have to look carefully at the letters to distinguish the odd word out.

Drawing

Read the word under each picture.

flower   sun   apple   balloon

Now look at the words under these boxes. Draw a picture to go with each word.

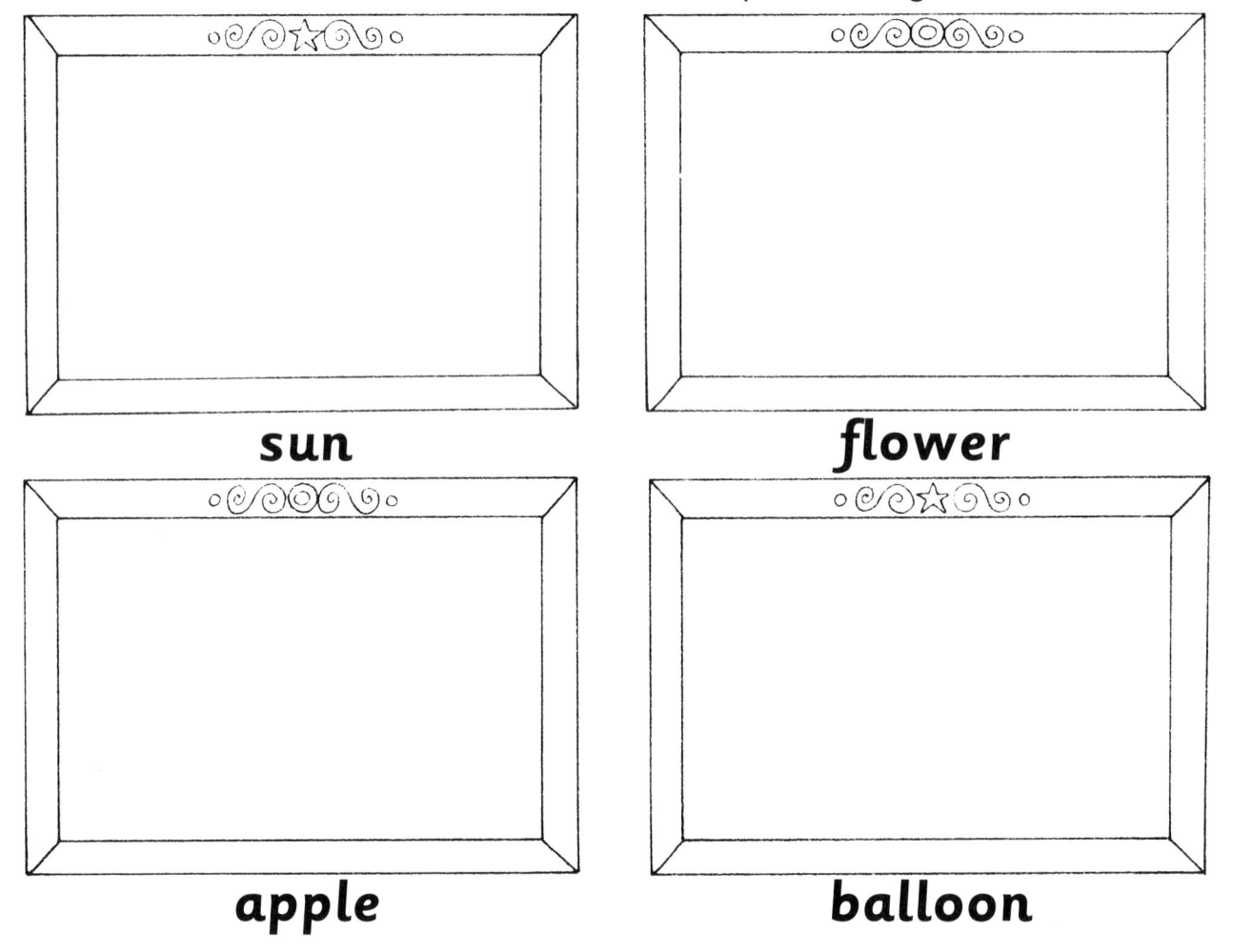

sun

flower

apple

balloon

Some children will identify the word by its first letter and some by its shape. Either way, they will have taken an important step forward in learning to read.

Tell a story

Look at the pictures. What is happening? Tell the story to a grown-up.

Encourage your child to look carefully at each picture and describe what is happening. Try to get them to use as many different words as possible, by asking lots of questions.

Can you?

What can you do?

Put a tick ✓ in the circle if you can, put a cross ✗ if you can't.

Can you skip? ◯

Can you ride a bike? ◯

Can you hop? ◯

Can you swim? ◯

Can you rollerskate? ◯

Can you count to 10? ◯

Can you write your name? ◯

Can you jump? ◯

Children will feel they have read these simple sentences, even if they worked it out simply by looking at the pictures. Success is a great motivator, so don't forget to give plenty of encouragement.

What next?

Can you work out which is the last picture in each of the stories? Draw a line from the empty box to the missing picture.

Predicting what happens next is an important reading skill - for adults as well as children!

Spot the word

Look at each picture and say its name. Then choose the right label and colour it blue.

cat	dog

car	jar

lion	tiger

ball	doll

book	duck

wig	windmill

bee	banana

dog	dinosaur

egg	elephant

In the first five examples your child will probably choose the word by recognising its first letter. The rest of the word pairs have the same initial letter, which makes the exercise harder, but one word is short and the other is long. Encourage your child to think about whether a word <u>sounds</u> short or long, and to see that this often relates to how it <u>looks</u>.

Finish the pictures

Make these faces **happy**  or **sad** .

happy   sad   happy   sad

Colour the bow-ties **red** 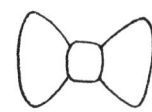 or **blue** .

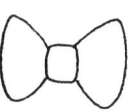

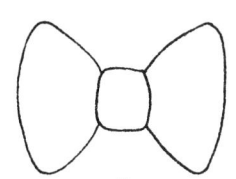

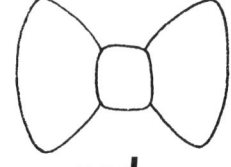

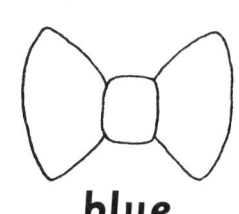

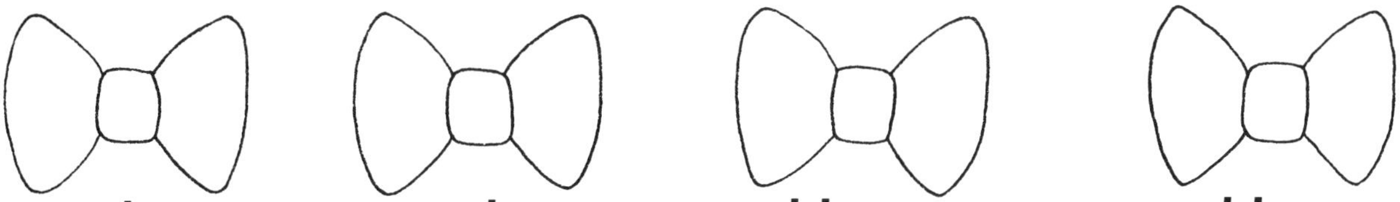

red   red   blue   blue

Decorate the hat with **stripes**  or **spots** .

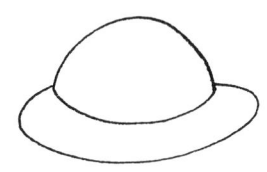

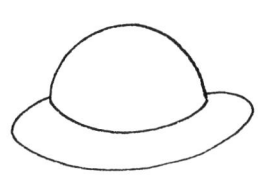

spots   stripes   stripes   spots

Add **curly**  or **straight**  hair.

curly   curly   curly   straight

Help your child to colour the red and blue bowties in the instructions first. Make sure they understand that the word under each face tells them what to draw. Following instructions is a very useful reading skill.

Rhymes

Read the words and try to find a rhyme for each one, like carrot/parrot. Join the rhymes with a line.

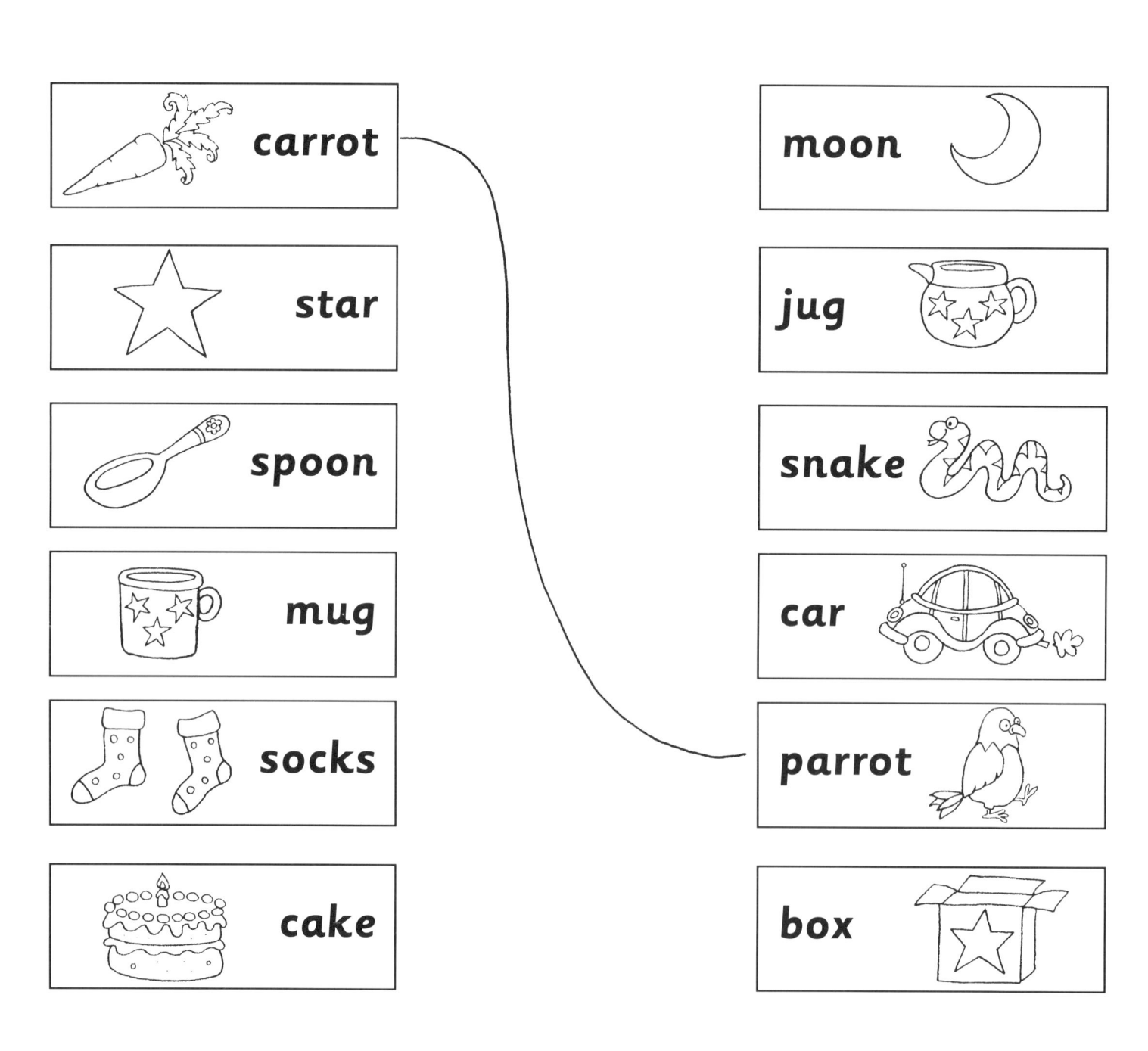

carrot	moon
star	jug
spoon	snake
mug	car
socks	parrot
cake	box

Very young children often have an excellent grasp of rhyme. They may also notice that words that rhyme are not always spelt the same way.

Opposites

Look at the mug. It is hot. Can you see something cold? Join the two pictures with a line. Now draw lines to join the other opposites. Use a different colour each time.

hot   **asleep**   **happy**   **open**   **big**

shut   **awake**   **little**   **cold**   **sad**

This exercise will help your child with word recognition.

Doris Duck

[duck] lived on a [pond], in a [field] with a flock of [sheep]. One [sun] day [duck] went for a walk. [duck] walked away from the pond, across the [field], past the [sheep] and under the [gate]. [duck] stopped to eat some [bread] with the [chickens], had a quick drink from a [bucket], and went to look at the new [piglets]. Near the [house] [duck] was chased by a [dog] and hissed at by a [cat]. So [duck] waddled quickly across a [bridge] and under another [gate], and found she was back in her own [field] with the [sheep].

Look at the picture of the farm. Use your finger to show where [duck] walked.

Where did [duck] see a [wheelbarrow] a [pram] and a [tractor] ?

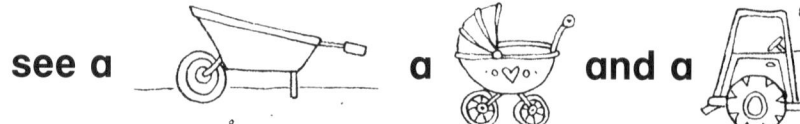

Picture stories are a good way to boost your child's confidence, by making them feel as if they are reading. Your child is also learning to follow instructions.

Safari park signs

Can you read all the safari park signs?
Which road would you take to see the tigers?
Is the shop open or closed?
Where would you go to buy an ice-cream?
Which car is just arriving and which is just leaving?

elephants   tigers
giraffes
car park
way in
shop

danger

picnic area

ice cream

way out

open

Encourage your child to notice signs when you're out – both pictorial and written. There are many different kinds of letter forms, so they need to learn to recognise a wide range of styles. This exercise also tests your child's observation and logic.

Riddles

Each animal has lost its balloon. Draw a string to join each balloon to the right animal, using the riddles to help you.

I am brown, and I squeak, and I am very small. Some people don't seem to like me at all!
Who am I?

I am big and I am gentle, and I am useful to you. The milk that I give can make other things too.
Who am I?

I am quite big and hairy, I growl and I bark. My favourite thing is a walk in the park.
Who am I?

I am big and grey, with a very long nose which I use as a hand as well as a hose.
Who am I?

Your child will need you to read out the riddles, but see if they can work the answers out for themselves. The clues are not intended to be difficult, but will help them learn how words can be used to build up a picture of something - and that reading is fun!